It's Easy To Play The Sixties.

Wise Publications
London/New York/Sydney/Cologne

Exclusive distributors:
Music Sales Limited
8/9 Frith Street, London W1V 5TZ, England.
Music Sales Pty Limited
120 Rothschild Avenue, Rosebery, NSW 2018, Australia.

This book © Copyright 1988 by
Wise Publications
UK ISBN 0.7119.1326.9
Order No. AM68347

Art direction by Mike Bell
Cover illustration Paul Allen
Arranged by Frank Booth
Compiled by Peter Evans

Music Sales' complete catalogue lists thousands
of titles and is free from your local music
shop, or direct from Music Sales Limited.
Please send £1 in stamps for postage to
Music Sales Limited, 8/9 Frith Street, London W1V 5TZ.

Printed in the United Kingdom by
Eyre & Spottiswoode Limited, London and Margate.

Nights In White Satin

Words & Music by Justin Hayward

I can't say an - y - more. _____ 'Cause I love you. _ Yes, I

you'll be in the end, _____ and I

F   Em   A

to Coda ⊕

love you, _ oh, how I love _you _____

C   Em   D   Em   D

Em   D   C   B

D.𝄋 al ⊕

Em   D   C   B   C   B

⊕ CODA

love ___ you. _____

rit.

Em   D   Em

5

Love Is Blue
(L'Amour Est Bleu)

Music by Andre Popp
Original Words by Pierre Cour
English Lyric by Bryan Blackburn

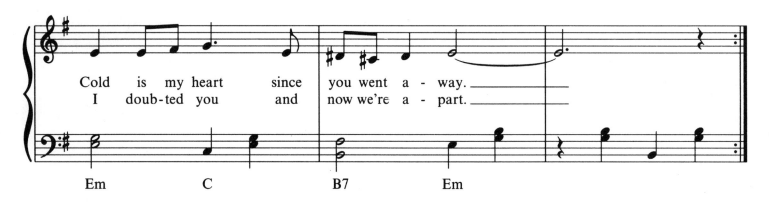

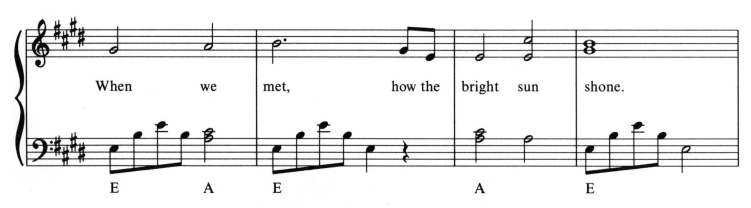

Then love died, now the rain - bow is gone.

G#m   A6   B7   E

Black, black, the nights I've known, long - ing for you, so

Em   A   D   G   Em   C

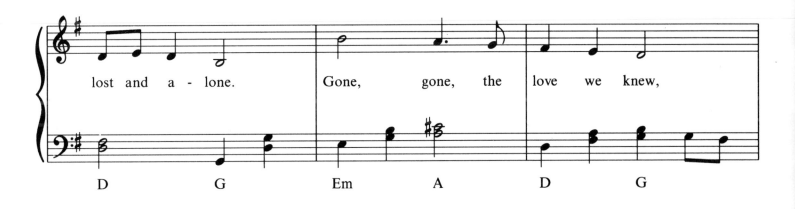

lost and a - lone. Gone, gone, the love we knew,

D   G   Em   A   D   G

blue is my world, now

1 I'm with-out you. _____

2 I'm with-out you.
rit.

Em   C   B7   Em   B7   Em

I (Who Have Nothing)

Words by Jerry Leiber & Mike Stoller
Music by C. Donida

The Girl From Ipanema
(Garota De Ipanema)

Original Words by Vinicius De Moraes English Lyric by Norman Gimbel
Music by Antonio Carlos Jobim

Moderate Bossa nova

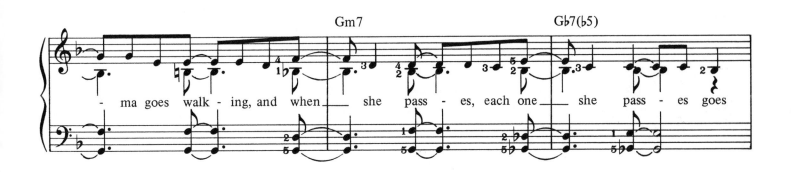

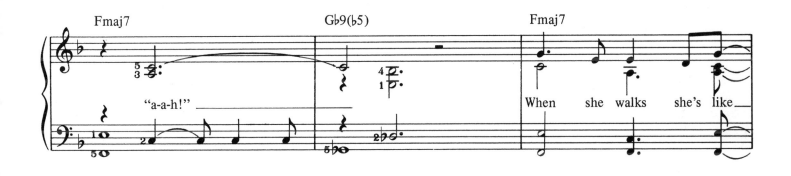

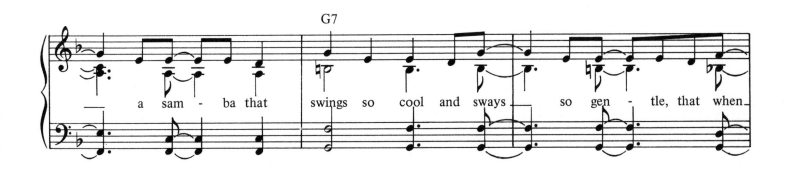

Somethin' Stupid

Words & Music by C. Carson Parks

And then I go and spoil it all by say-in' some-thin' stu-pid like, "I

1.
love you." I can love you."

2.

See it in your eyes that you des - pise the same old lines you heard the

night be - fore. And though it's just a line to you, for

me it's true and nev - er seemed so right be - fore. I

One Note Samba
(Samba De Uma Nota So)

Original Words by N. Mendonca English Lyric by Jon Hendricks
Music by Antonio Carlos Jobim

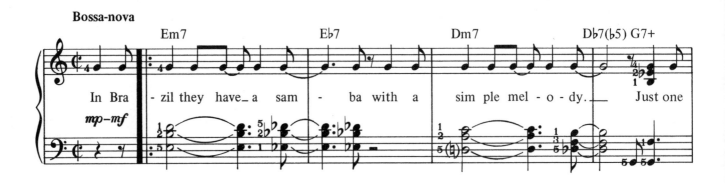

In Bra -zil they have_ a sam - ba with a sim ple mel - o - dy.__ Just one

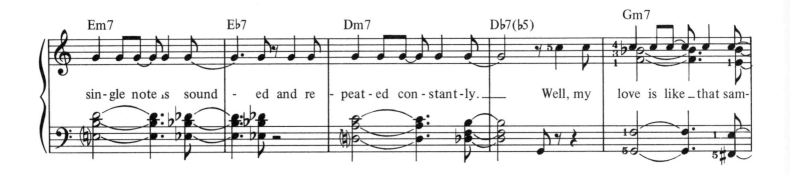

sin - gle note is sound - ed and re - peat - ed con - stant-ly.__ Well, my love is like _ that sam-

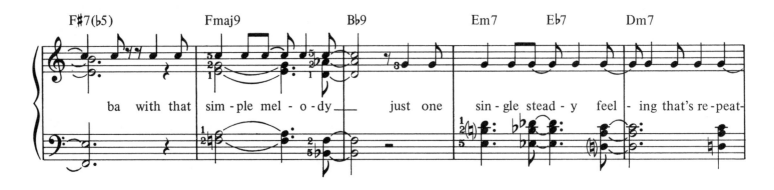

ba with that sim - ple mel - o - dy__ just one sin - gle stead - y feel - ing that's re - peat-

ed constant-ly.__ That's the way my love is like the sun that shines a-bove is ev - er

A Whiter Shade Of Pale

Words & Music by Keith Reid & Gary Brooker

He Ain't Heavy He's My Brother

Words by Bob Russell
Music by Bobby Scott

If I'm la - den at all,___ I'm la - den with sad - ness___ that

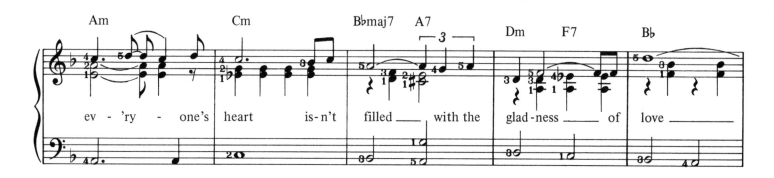

ev - 'ry - one's heart is - n't filled ___ with the glad - ness ___ of love ___

D.%. al Coda ✙ *CODA*

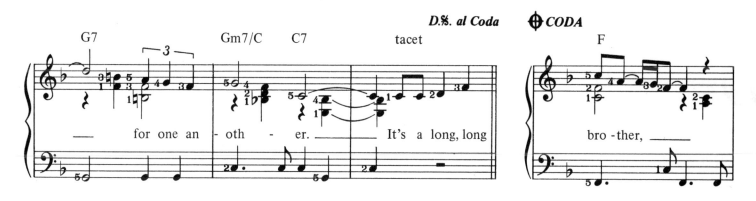

___ for one an - oth - er. ___ It's a long, long

bro - ther, ___

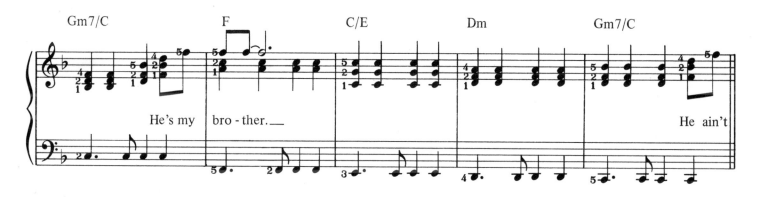

He's my bro - ther.___ He ain't

Repeat to Fade

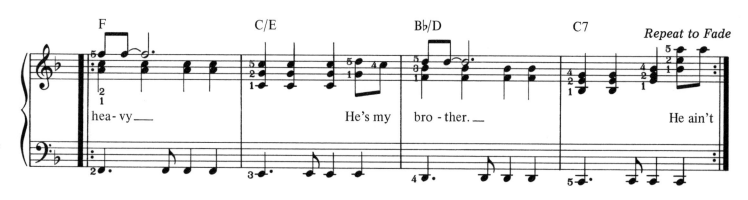

hea - vy___ He's my bro - ther. ___ He ain't

21

The Boxer

Words & Music by Paul Simon

Moderately

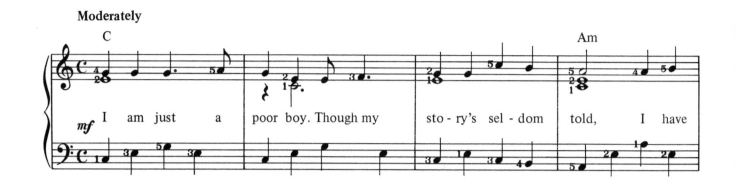

I am just a poor boy. Though my sto-ry's sel - dom told, I have

squan - dered my re - sis - tance for a pock - et - ful of mum-bles, such are

pro - mi - ses. ___ All lies and jest, still a

man hears what he wants to hear, ___ And dis - re - gards the rest. ___

When I left my home and my fam-i-ly,— I was no more than a boy in the com-pa-ny— of stran-gers in the qui-et of a rail-way sta-tion run-ning scared.— Lay-ing low, seek-ing out the poor-er quar-ters where the

rag - ged peo-ple go, look-ing for the pla-ces on - ly they would know.

Lie - la - lie, lie - la lie la lie la

lie lie - la - lie. Lie la lie la la la la lie __

__ la la la la lie. ___

Ask-ing on - ly work-man's wag - es I come look - ing for a

job, but I get no of - fers, _____ just a come on from the

whores _ on Sev - enth Av - en - ue. _____ I do de -

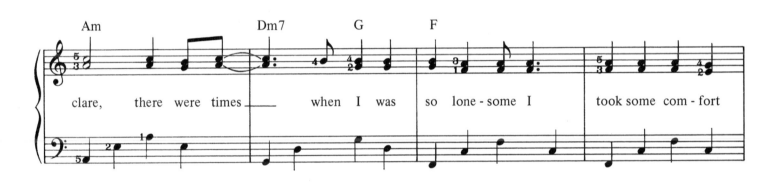

clare, there were times _____ when I was so lone - some I took some com - fort

there. Ooo la la _ la la _ la la. _

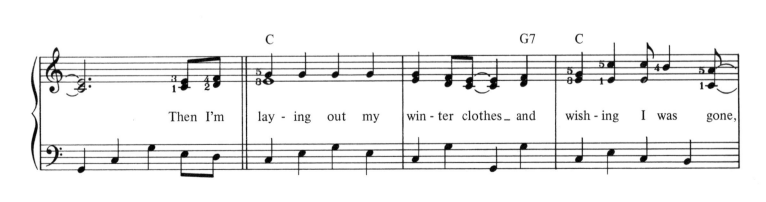

Then I'm lay - ing out my win - ter clothes _ and wish - ing I was gone,

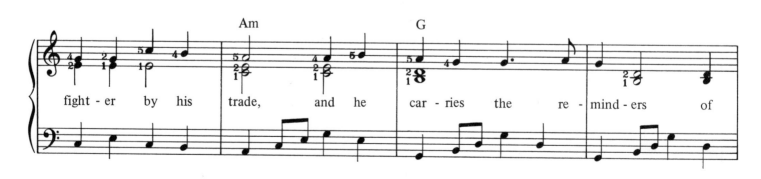

Streets Of London

Words & Music by Ralph McTell

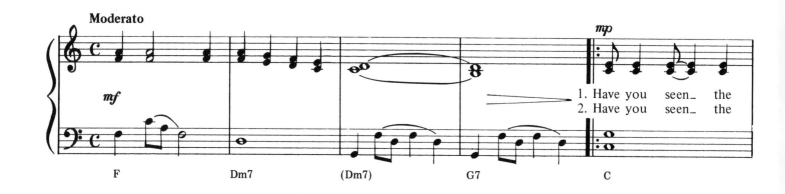

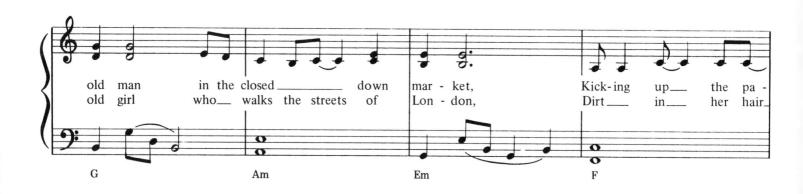

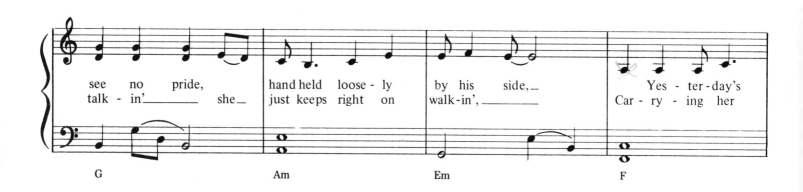

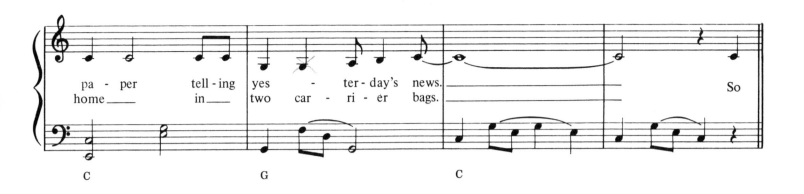

pa - per tell - ing yes - ter - day's news.\
home ___ in ___ two car - ri - er bags. So

C   G   C

CHORUS

how can you tell ___ me you're lone - ly,   And say for you

F   C   G7   Am   D

___ that the sun don't shine? ___   Let me take you by the hand and

G7   C   G

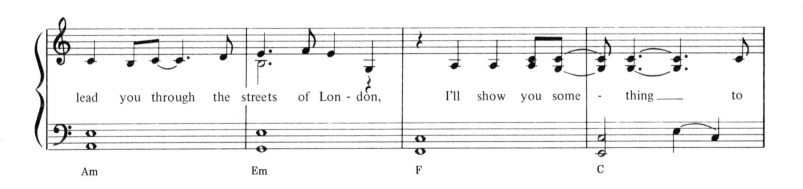

lead you through the streets of Lon - don,   I'll show you some - thing ___ to

Am   Em   F   C

1.

make you change your mind.

G7   C   G   Am   Dm7   G7

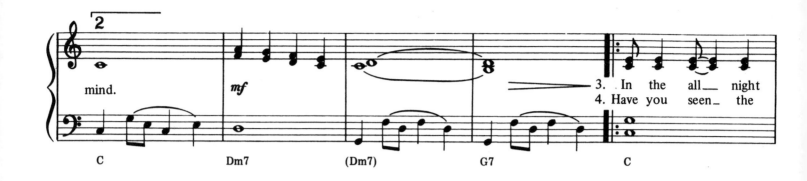

mind.   *mf*   3. In the all__ night
                                                         4. Have you seen__ the

C   Dm7   (Dm7)   G7   C

ca - fé   at a   quar - ter past__ e - lev - en,   Same old__ man
old man   out - side the sea - man's miss - ion,   Mem-'ry fa - ding with__

G   Am   Em   F

__   sit - ting there   on his   own,__   Look-ing at__ the
__   the me - dal   rib - bons that he   wears?__   In our win - ter

C   D   G7   C

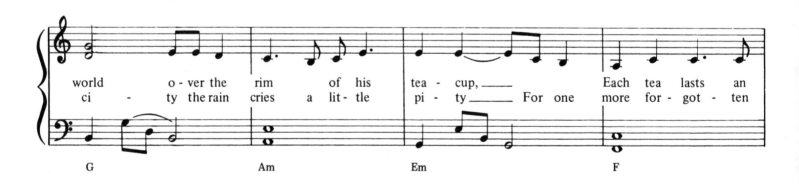

world   o - ver the   rim   of his   tea - cup,__   Each tea lasts an
ci - ty the rain   cries a lit - tle   pi - ty__ For one more for - got - ten

G   Am   Em   F

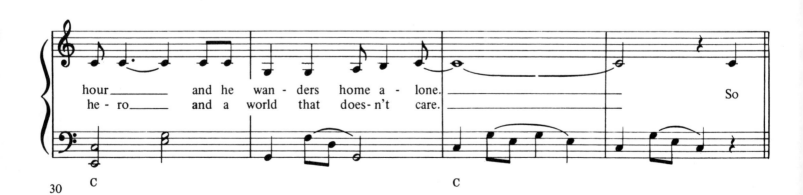

hour__   and he wan - ders home a - lone.__   So
he - ro__   and a world that does-n't care.__

C   C

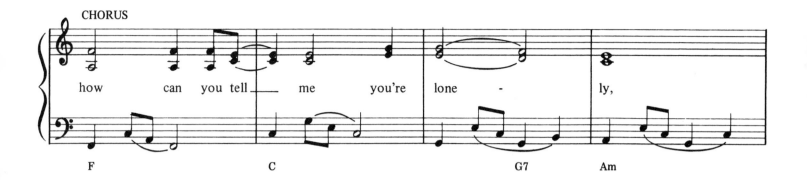

how   can   you tell   me   you're   lone - ly,

F   C   G7   Am

And   say   for   you   that   the   sun   don't   shine?

D   G7

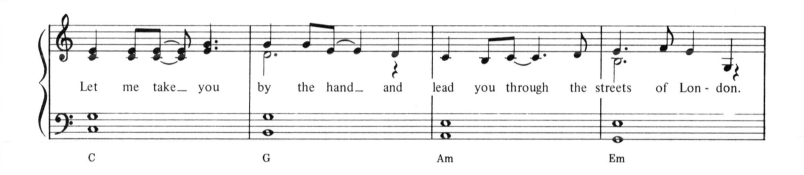

Let   me   take   you   by   the   hand   and   lead   you   through   the   streets   of Lon - don.

C   G   Am   Em

1

I'll   show   you   some - thing   to   make   you   change   your   mind.

F   C   G7   C

2

mind.

G   Am   Dm   G7   C

Homeward Bound

Words & Music by Paul Simon

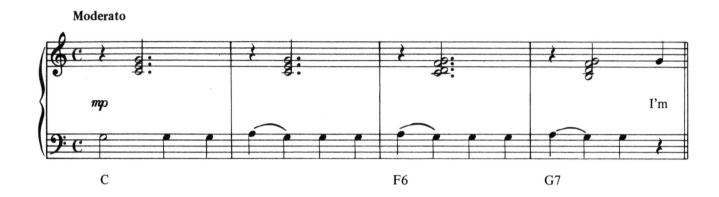

Moderato

I'm

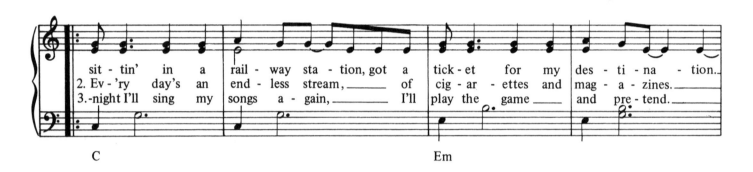

sit - tin' in a rail - way sta - tion, got a tick - et for my des - ti - na - tion.
2. Ev - 'ry day's an end - less stream, of cig - ar - ettes and mag - a - zines.
3. -night I'll sing my songs a - gain, I'll play the game and pre - tend.

Mm On a tour of
Mm And each town looks the
Mm But all my words come

one night stands, my suit - case and gui - tar in hand and ev - 'ry stop is
same to me, the mov - ies and the fac - tor - ries and ev - 'ry strang - er's
back to me in shades of med - i - oc - ri - ty like emp - ti - ness in

neat - ly planned _ for a | po - et   and   a | one - man band. _____
face I see _____ re - | minds me   that   I | long _ to   be. _____
har - mo - ny _____ I | need some - one to com - | fort   me. _____

CHORUS

Home - ward _ bound,   I wish I was, _____ Home - ward _ bound. _____

C   F   C   F

_____ Home,   where my thought's_ es - cap-ing, Home, where my mu - sic's play - ing,

C   Dm C B♭ F C   Dm C B♭ F

Home,   where my love _ lies wait - ing, si - lent - ly   for me. _____

2. —
3. To

C   Dm C B♭ F G7   C

3.

rall.

_____ si - lent - ly   for   me.

C   Cmaj 7   G   C7   C   F6   C

Something

Words & Music by George Harrison

Yesterday

Words & Music by John Lennon & Paul McCartney

Moderato

mp

Yes - ter - day,   All   my   trou - bles seemed so   far   a - way,
Sud - den - ly,   I'm not half the man I   used   to be,

F   Em7   A7   Dm   Dm7

Now it looks as though they're here to stay. ___ Oh I be - lieve ___ in
There's a sha - dow hang - ing ov - er me, ___ Oh Yes - ter - day ___ came

Bb   C7   F   C   Dm7   G7

Yes - ter - day. ___ }   Why   she   had   to   go   I   don't
sud - den - ly. ___ }

Bb   F   Em7   A7   Dm   C   Bb   Dm

know. She would - n't   say.   I   said

Gm   Cm   F   Em7   A7

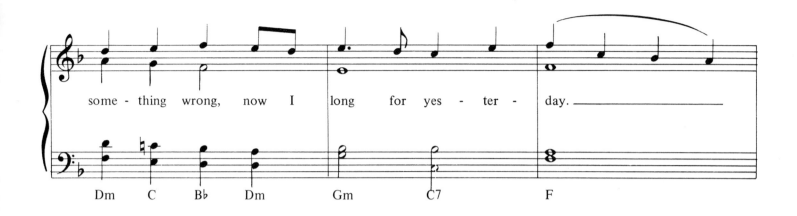

some - thing wrong, now I long for yes - ter - day. _____

Dm C B♭ Dm Gm C7 F

Yes - ter - day, Love was such an eas - y game to play,

Em7 A7 Dm

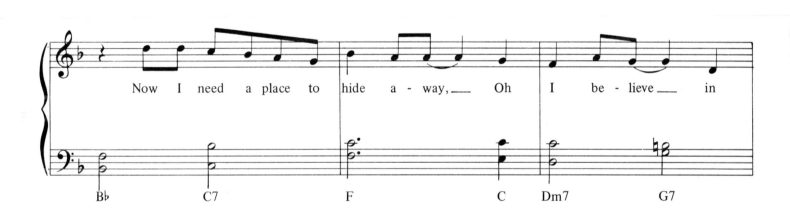

Now I need a place to hide a - way,___ Oh I be - lieve___ in

B♭ C7 F C Dm7 G7

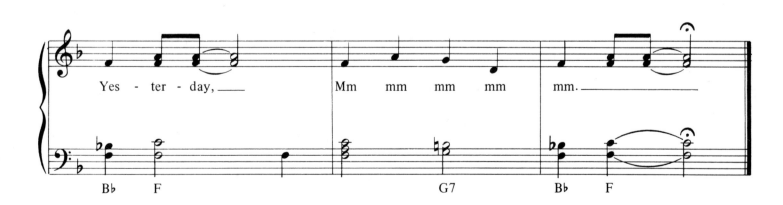

Yes - ter - day,___ Mm mm mm mm mm. _____

B♭ F G7 B♭ F

This Guy's In Love With You

Words by Hal David
Music by Burt Bacharach

Sunny

Words & Music by Bobby Hebb

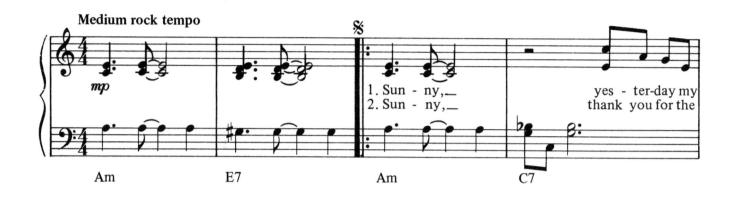

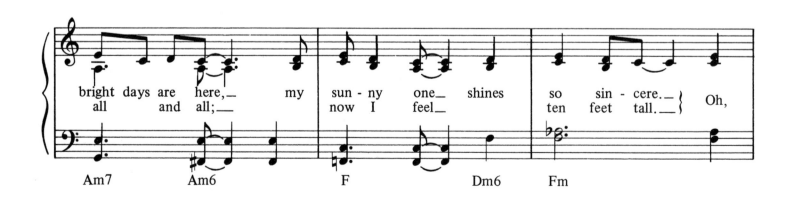

sun - ny one so true,____ I love you.____

Bm7−5   E7   Am   E7

Sun - ny,____ thank you for the truth you've let me see.
Sun - ny,____ thank you for that smile up - on your face.

Am   C7   F   F7   E7

Sun - ny, thank you for the facts from A to Z. My
Sun - ny, thank you for that gleam that flows with grace.

Am   C7   F   F7   E7

life____ was torn____ like____ wind-blown sand,____Then a rock was formed____when we held hands.
You're____my spark____ of____ na - ture's fire;____ You're my sweet____com - plete de - sire.____

Am   Am7   Am6   F   Dm6   Fm

After repeat
D.S. and fade

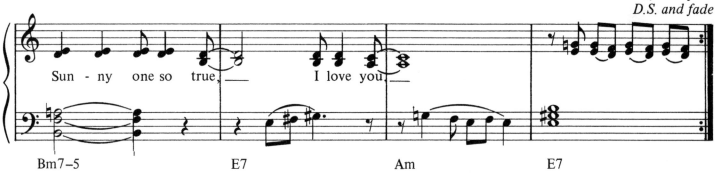

Sun - ny one so true,____ I love you.____

Bm7−5   E7   Am   E7

Eleanor Rigby

Words & Music by John Lennon & Paul McCartney

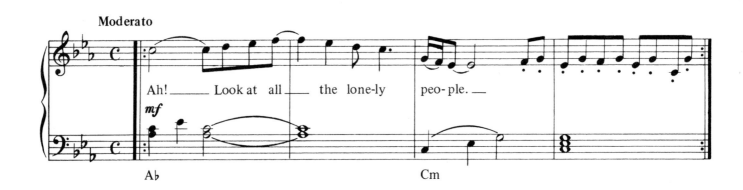

Ah!____ Look at all____ the lone-ly peo-ple.____

A♭   Cm

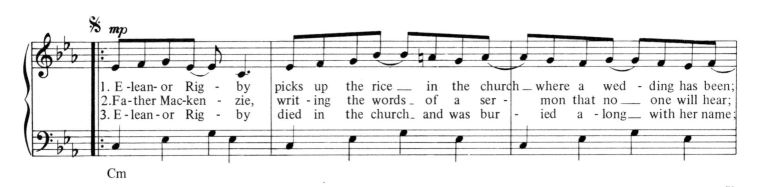

1. E-lean-or Rig - by picks up the rice____ in the church____ where a wed - ding has been;
2. Fa-ther Mac-ken - zie, writ - ing the words____ of a ser - mon that no____ one will hear;
3. E-lean-or Rig - by died in the church____ and was bur - ied a - long____ with her name;

Cm

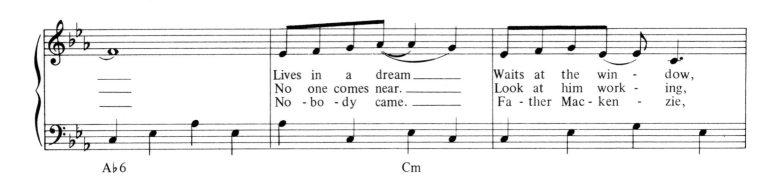

Lives in a dream____ Waits at the win - dow,
No one comes near.____ Look at him work - ing,
No-bo-dy came.____ Fa - ther Mac - ken - zie,

A♭6   Cm

wear-ing the face____ that she keeps____ in a jar____ by the door.
darn-ing his socks____ in the night____ when there's no - bo-dy there.
wip-ing the dirt____ from his hands____ as he walks from the grave.

A♭6

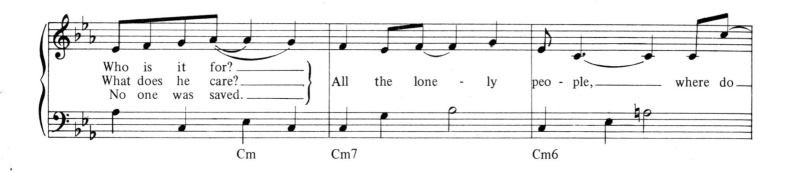

Who is it for? _____
What does he care? _____
No one was saved. _____

All the lone - ly peo - ple, _____ where do _____

Cm   Cm7   Cm6

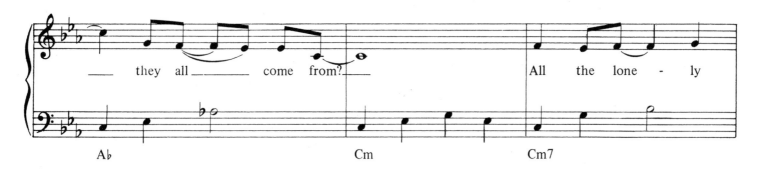

_____ they all _____ come from? _____

All the lone - ly

Ab   Cm   Cm7

Last time to Coda ⊕

peo - ple, _____ where do _____ they all _____ be - long. _____

Cm6   Ab   Cm

D. S. al Coda

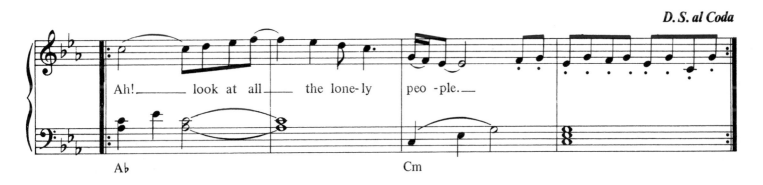

Ah! _____ look at all _____ the lone-ly peo - ple. _____

Ab   Cm

⊕ *CODA*

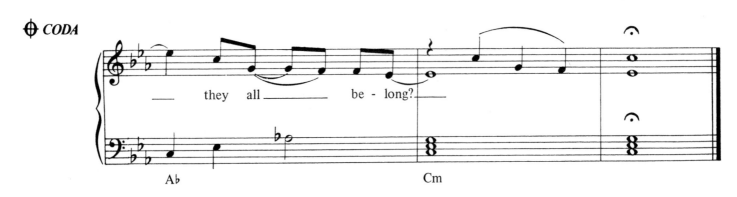

_____ they all _____ be - long? _____

Ab   Cm

43

Norwegian Wood

Words & Music by John Lennon & Paul McCartney

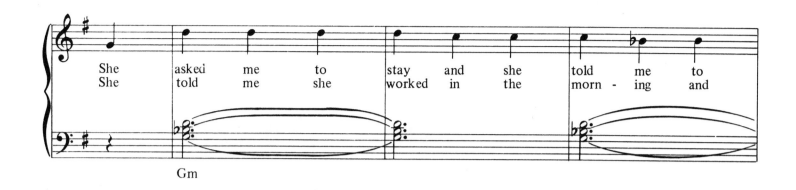

She asked me to stay and she told me to
She told me to she worked in the morning to and

Gm

sit an - y - where. _____
start - ed to laugh. _____

C

____ So I looked a - round and I no - ticed there
____ I told her I did - n't and crawled off to

Gm

2nd time D.C. al Fine

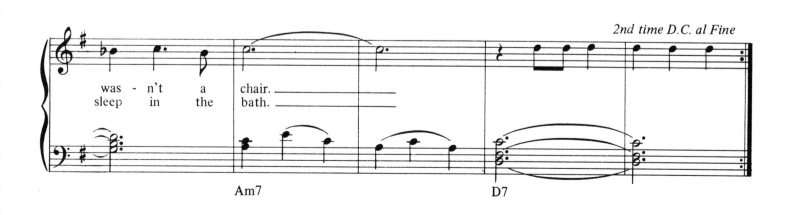

was - n't a chair. _____
sleep in the bath. _____

Am7   D7

45

If My Friends Could See Me Now

Words by Dorothy Fields
Music by Cy Coleman

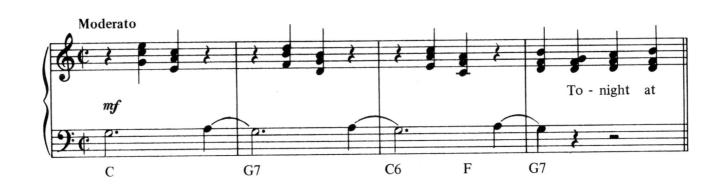

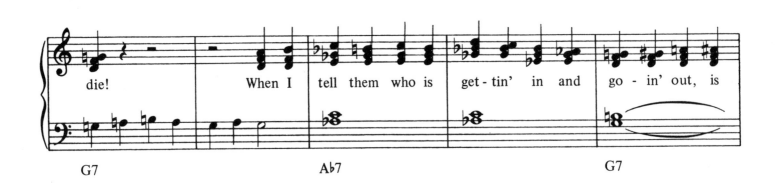

I. 1. If they could see me now, that lit - tle gang of mine,

C   C7

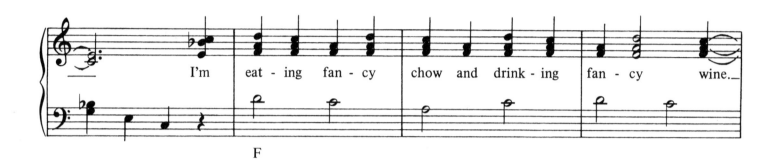

I'm eat - ing fan - cy chow and drink - ing fan - cy wine.

F

I'd like those stum - ble bums to see for a fact the kind of

B7   E   Am   E Am

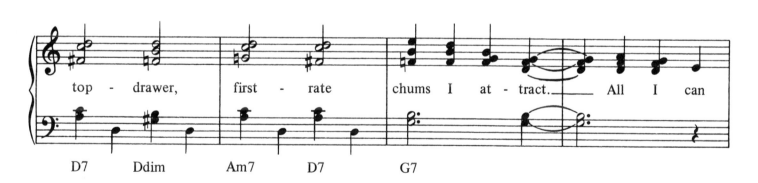

top - drawer, first - rate chums I at - tract. All I can

D7 Ddim Am7 D7 G7

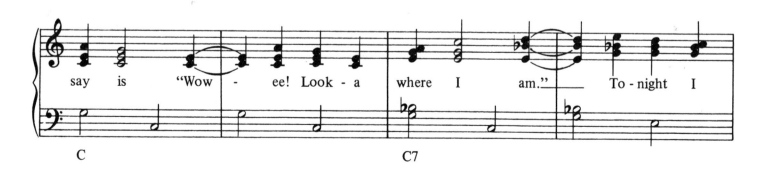

say is "Wow - ee! Look - a where I am." To - night I

C   C7

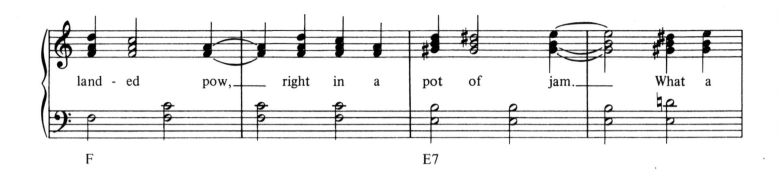

land - ed pow,___ right in a pot of jam.___ What a

F   E7

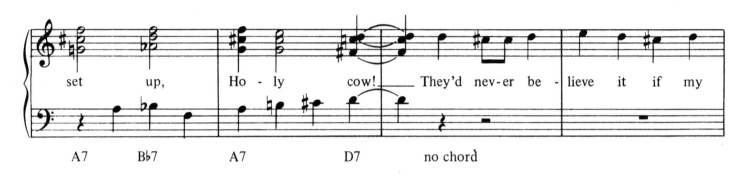

set up, Ho - ly cow!___ They'd nev-er be - lieve it if my

A7   Bb7   A7   D7   no chord

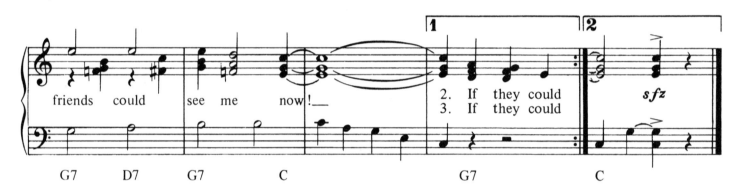

1

friends could see me now!___   2. If they could
                           3. If they could

2

sfz

G7   D7   G7   C   G7   C

2. If they could see me now,
   My little dusty group,
   Traipsin' round this million dollar chicken coop.
   I'd hear those thrift shop cats say: "Brother, get her!
   Draped on a bedspread made from three kinds of fur."
   All I can say is "Wow!
   Wait till the riff and raff
   See just exactly how he signed this autograph."
   What a build-up, Holy cow!
   They'd never believe it, if my friends could see me now.

3. If they could see me now,
   Alone with Mr V.,
   Who's waitin' on me like he was a maitre d'.
   I hear my buddies saying, "Crazy, what gives?
   Tonight she's living like the other half lives."
   To think the highest brow,
   Which I must say is he,
   Should pick the lowest brow, which there's no doubt is me.
   What a step up, Holy cow!
   They'd never believe it, if my friends could see me now.